The Thrill Of The Chase

How to thrive in singledom, become a better man and get the girls you actually want

ISBN: 1974453308
ISBN-13: 978-1974453306

FREE STUFF

For a free electronic version of the book
Email joe@thelondondater.co.uk with a photo of yourself holding the
physical copy.

For 7 unique, fun London date ideas emailed to you every week
www.thelondondater.co.uk/dates

For a comprehensive list of the best cheap nights out in London
www.thelondondater.co.uk/nightsout

For expert tips on reducing your fear of speaking to women
www.thelondondater.co.uk/how-to-be-fearless

For a list of Tinder hacks to take your online dating to the next level
www.thelondondater.co.uk/tinder-hacks

This is a true story, although many names have been changed.

Thanks to Alex White, Ana Maria Tolbaru, Bostjan Belingar, Ciaran Callam Farhana Mangera, Gloria Wright, James Davies, Jeff Winch, Katrina Bushby, Laura Nineham, Matt Rudnitsky, Rachel Froment and Tom Badley for helping bring this book to life.

CONTENTS

INTRODUCTION

This book will teach you how to love being single, and as a result:

- attract an abundance of beautiful women into your life
- become more confident, ambitious, fearless and socially savvy
- eventually get the girlfriend you always wanted.

It explains the process that thousands of men have successfully used to improve their sex lives. If you copy it, you can do the same.

This process is centred around learning to truly enjoy the thrill of the chase. It sounds simple. Sometimes it is. Other times, it'll be the hardest thing you teach yourself to do.

When I discovered this process, I was going through the longest dry spell of my life. I'd been stuck in a relationship I hated, but stayed in because I didn't think I could do any better. I had my heart broken after being dumped (and probably cheated on) on Christmas Day. My strategy for meeting a new girlfriend was to go out, get wasted and hope for the best.

The book starts off with a few embarrassing stories, such as how I unsuccessfully pursued the fat girl from school, then peppered her phone with desperate text messages. You'll learn all about the money I wasted on match.com and eHarmony before online dating had even become cool.

Thankfully, there was a turning point. The book explains how I taught myself to become better with women, without having to get hammered or spend hours swiping on Tinder.

You'll hear all the key lessons I learned along the way, including the foolproof method for finding a girlfriend you'll love forever.

The story finishes with five crazy sex stories that occurred as a result of my new-found seduction skills.

This is no magic pill. As with any emotional transformation, it's a tough road to tread. You'll probably want to give up more than once.

Still, if you're tired of trying to 'get lucky' with women who are 'out of your league', I'd recommend following the path outlined in the pages ahead.

Enjoy the book,

Joe.

1. MY YEAR NOT GETTING LAID

True love. We humans need it as much as air and water.

As infants, we're almost fearless. We'll scream, laugh or cry without caring what people think. We'll drink bleach or run into busy roads if you let us.

Yet, from the earliest age, we're terrified of losing our parents' affection. It's the first thing we learn to fear. Toddlers instinctively alter their behaviour when their parents become angry. It's biological. Some studies even suggest a lack of parental love can stunt your growth.

This longing to be loved never disappears.

Once puberty arrives, we obsess over our classroom crushes. We crave their admiration. We're devastated when it turns out they fancy someone else. It might not be as damaging as being shunned by Mum and Dad, but a lack of puppy love can also cause lasting emotional damage.

While we can typically control these emotions better as adults, true love remains what we're all looking for.

'Falling' in love

There are millions of books, songs and poems that tell us what love is.

A stereotypical English lad like myself loves his family, best friends and local football team in different ways.

However, there are just two types of romantic love.

- Falling in love
- Jumping in love

Both feel fantastic, but one is far healthier than the other.

Falling in love feels like an obsession. This perfect princess is forever in your thoughts. She's your 'everything'. You'll do anything to keep hold of her. You're addicted to these happy, light-headed goofy emotions.

I've been in love with four women. The first three I definitely 'fell' for.

For Gemma, I fell hard. She was far from perfect. In fact, she had obvious physical flaws and intense family issues. These should have been red flags. It's funny how your brain ignores these when you've 'fallen'.

Instead, your attention focuses only on what you're attracted to. In this case, her chocolate eyes, cute smile and huge boobs.

However, people don't 'fall' in love with physical features. I actually loved how Gemma made me feel important. She pined after me and told me I was handsome. She was game for regular sex. For the average guy who doesn't have much else going on, that's usually all it takes.

After hearing of her family troubles, it was nice to make her feel needed. It felt meaningful being her knight in shining armour. We went on romantic getaways. We moved into a small flat by the beach. Life appeared peachy.

Sadly, these troubles ultimately caught up with her. Soon after moving in, she was diagnosed with manic depression. Small arguments would turn into crying and screaming. Minor disagreements became broken ornaments. Panic attacks, insults and slaps were soon the norm.

I gave all I could to help her. Cuddles, gifts, supportive words. Nevertheless, these episodes pushed us to a breaking point.

Falling in love is like a balloon inflated with morphine. You float through life feeling goofy and dizzy. Our balloon was slowly polluted with toxic fumes for the best part of a year.

It finally popped on Christmas Day.

The nightmare before Christmas

Getting really drunk and going clubbing on Christmas Eve is a dumb idea. Still, my group of school friends go to the same club every year.

On this occasion, Gemma went missing for the entire evening. When the confetti dropped and Mariah Carey welcomed midnight, she was nowhere to be seen. Eventually, we found her, and I thought nothing of it.

She was quiet for the whole of Christmas Day though, and not just because of her hangover. Before we went to bed, she admitted she spent the night snogging some idiot in the corner of the club.

My heart fell flat. How could this have happened!? The argument lasted hours. I wanted her out of the house. She was begging to stay, but it was a lost battle. She could see how deep she'd cut me.

Suddenly, her ringtone broke the silence. Her phone lit up, still with an image of us snuggling on the sofa. It was him. Her face lit up just as brightly. She didn't think twice about answering. I'll never forget the smirk on her face when my whole world came crashing down.

"Hi!" she beamed proudly.

I could hear his voice. He invited her over. Clearly, he was unaware of the drama taking place in our flat of nearly two years.

"Sure," she said without hesitation, making eye contact that twisted a knife in my spine.

It was past midnight, but off she went. Just like that. As she jumped in the car, I shouted obscenities out the window.

My everything was on her way to have a one-night stand.

A subtle heartbreak

Poor concentration, broken sleep, binge eating. All classic symptoms of a break-up.

A loss of dopamine, the happy hormone released when we're around someone we love, can result in cravings similar to those experienced by drug addicts. We miss our exes like smackheads miss heroin.

The brain responds by releasing an added dose of the stress hormone, cortisol. This is why heartbroken people often feel tired with no motivation, heavy muscles and a tense chest. Thinking about your ex activates the same section of the brain that registers physical pain.

I didn't notice these symptoms. I thought I was relieved at being free from Gemma's episodes. I was out meeting women and boasting how I couldn't wait to sleep with someone different. Deep down, all I actually wanted was for someone else to make me feel special like she did.

I couldn't see it, but this neediness was repelling every woman I encountered. There's nothing stinkier to women than desperation, and I was doused head-to-toe in it. Although I didn't tell anyone I was heartbroken, it was impossible to hide. Women are brilliant at reading body language. To them, it was written all over me.

This neediness shone brightest when women would actually show interest. Shortly after becoming single, I took home this fat girl who was a goth at my secondary school, tried for something to happen in the bedroom and became visually butthurt when she wanted to leave. For the next few days, I polluted her phone with pathetic text messages.

There was also this 19-year-old tattooed girl I'd met at the same grunge club. I had dinner with her at a fancy seaside restaurant and got unnecessarily excited at everything she said.

"You're studying art? Amazing!"
"You're off to university this summer? Wow, that's so cool!"

I still remember the fear in her eyes when I said I couldn't wait to see her again. I only dated one other girl that entire year.

When things got really desperate, I paid for a monthly subscription to match.com and took the infamous 436-question eHarmony personality test. This was before Tinder made online dating cool. Back then, it was only for older people who were serious about settling down with a partner.

I was subscribed to these websites for six months. Not one date from either of them.

Reality TV romance

In January 2014, I was invited to appear on the Channel 4 reality show, 'First Dates'. A popular fly-on-the-wall series that pairs two singletons on a dinner date at Paternoster Chop House in St. Paul's.

I'd just been offered a new job in London as well, so I had a couple of events to look forward to.

"Her name is Hannah. She's blonde, skinny, sort of quirky. She's so funny, Joe, and she works in the media! You'll love her," said the excitable casting agent a week before filming.

Brilliant. But what on earth would I do to impress this woman? I hadn't been on a successful date since the previous Christmas.

Once again, I turned to the internet. Not online dating sites this time, but dating advice. I discovered different types of routines and pick-up lines that would apparently make me more attractive.

I learned to palm-read. I practiced 'The Cube', an NLP routine from Neil Strauss' best-selling book, 'The Game'. I memorised some 'negs', another key concept from this book.

Wondering what it's like being filmed on a first date? I explain further in the final chapter. For now, all you need to know is how fit Hannah was. The researchers undersold her. She was already sitting at the table wearing a white buttoned-up shirt and trousers. Also, blonde shoulder-length hair with bright pink tips. Just my type.

She lapped up all the tricks I'd learned from the internet. She loved having her palm read. On several occasions, she laughed so loud that other daters turned around.

After we settled up, I dragged her past the production team, away from the free taxis home and into some other nearby bar.

The evening continued at The Clapham Grand, then straight home to my new pad. She said my bedroom looked like a crack den, but couldn't even finish the insult before we were ripping each other's clothes off. It was frantic. Hours of flirting and sexual tension turned to the most savage sexual experience I'd ever had. The hottest chick I'd ever slept with.

The truth about 'The Game'

I woke up the next morning believing I had superpowers. From getting no girls in over a year to having an absolute stunner sleeping next to me?

It must have been the techniques I memorised. The men who invented them must be real-life magicians...

The routines written in the 'The Game' are actually somewhat useful. They're brilliant for getting a beautiful woman's attention. They're wonderful for making you stand out among other men. Yet, they're certainly not the key to a woman's heart.

There's actually plenty of reasons not to use them. For starters, they're inauthentic. You're constantly putting on a charade, pretending to be this confident dude. By doing so, you're self-communicating that 'being yourself' isn't enough to get a girl. That's an unhealthy long-term dating strategy.

It's also a bit deceitful. No-one likes a fraud, especially if they're trying to 'trick' their way into a woman's pants. I didn't understand this, nor would I have cared at the time.

Additionally, these techniques are useless for getting a girl to stick around. I found that out the hard way with Hannah. I may have put on enough of a show to sleep with her, but I was still that needy dude who was desperate for a girlfriend. Like a lovesick puppy, I peppered her with text messages, repeatedly trying to get her out on a second date. She stopped responding soon enough.

After realising I'd never see her again, I went back online to learn more about these seductive superpowers. What I discovered would change my life forever.

2. THE LONDON SEDUCTION SOCIETY

Dating advice for men on the internet runs deeper than you'd think. We're not just talking articles and blog posts, but forums and in-field videos too.

Back in 2014, one forum stood out above all the others; The London Seduction Society. Its members would attend nightclubs sober to practice their seduction skills and write about what happened. Some were professional dating coaches who made a living teaching others how to chat up women. The rest were blokes who wanted to get better at this.

In spite of its cringeworthy title, the forum fascinated me. The articles discussed what worked and what didn't when trying to attract the opposite sex. There was advice on what to say, but also fashion, fitness, the best clubs in London to meet women etc.

An eye-catching section was titled 'Lay Reports'. This was filled with detailed stories of how users seduced and slept with women they'd just met. The idea behind these is that you're more likely to remember how you won a woman over if you write it down. By posting it publicly, you're also helping others learn how to do it. My initial thoughts were that the women involved would be mortified to read these reports. (I suppose, having written a few of my own in the final chapter, it'd be hypocritical to criticise them.)

The most useful section was titled 'Find A Wingman'. Here, users would write who they were, where they liked to go out, and the type of dude they wanted to 'wing' with. Essentially, they were inviting complete strangers to the club to help them chat up women. This concept fried my skull.

I was resistant to meeting strangers from the internet. This wasn't even Twitter or Facebook. There were no pictures, not even names. Just aliases like Diamond, Chips, Dante26. It felt so sketchy. I'd be embarrassed to be caught reading these lay reports, let alone partying with the authors.

Still, I was aware that meeting these men might help me get more girls like Hannah, and we all know the lengths that guys will go to get laid...

The Saturday Sarge

In the 'Find A Wingman' section, there was a sub-forum titled 'Events'. That's where I discovered The Saturday Sarge.

This was the weekly event where forum members would meet and chat up girls in large groups. ('Sarge' is a term that originated in 'The Game'. It means 'going out to hit on women').

Curiosity overwhelmed me.

The afternoon sarge started at 13.00 outside The Co-op in Covent Garden. Attendees stood out like a sore thumb. A group of 20 dudes stood in a circle, looking as awkward and embarrassed as I felt.

The group was split so three or four students would each sarge with one 'approach coach'. My coach, Jake, had long blonde hair and a softly spoken voice like a stereotypical hippie. His goal was to show us how to hit on women in the street.

None of the dudes in our group had ever tried this before. They were all easy enough to speak to. They seemed like normal men attempting an abnormal activity. No more awkward than your average dude. You'll learn how we got on later...

The evening sarge started at 20.00 outside O'Neills in Wardour Street. There weren't any approach coaches at this event. Just another bunch of average-looking blokes.

It was tougher getting to know these guys in a loud nightclub, but the novelty of being sober all night was something I'll never forget.

Usually, I'd need 3-4 beers inside me before finding the bravery to speak to a beautiful woman. Tonight was different.

Rather than give me stick for getting rejected by a girl, these guys would encourage it and ask what happened. I'd do the same to them. We'd joke, dance and flirt with so many women. This was just as fun as being drunk.

Although there was no epic sex story at the end of the evening, it was the most memorable night out I'd had in years. From that night, I was no longer nervous to make friends with people on these forums.

My 'wingmen'

Having since met hundreds of 'wingmen', I'd say there are typically two types of people willing to put serious time into getting better with women:

1. The anxious sociopath: Constantly nervous. Rarely smiles. Can't hold eye contact. Struggles to keep a conversation going. Terrified of speaking to women. I've met two or three of them, but I bet there are hundreds more who read all the articles, watch all the videos, but don't actually go out.

2. The completely normal bloke: He has a job, friends, hobbies and seems cool enough to speak to. He's just a bit useless with women. He probably struggles to speak to them at all if he's sober. If he does pluck up the courage, he crumbles after a couple of minutes or does something stupid to scare her away.

Most guys I've met fall into a third category though:

3. The absolute boss: These are the guys who have been studying the principles featured in this book for a while. They seem to have their shit together in all areas of life. They're charismatic, funny, the life of the party. Often, they're on top of their fashion and fitness. Many run their own business. They've learned that being attractive is not something you do; it's something you are. Some have become my best friends.

In February 2016, I also interviewed three of London's most famous dating coaches in a feature for AskMen. These were the guys writing most of the forum posts, as well as filming in-field footage demonstrating the best way to attract a female. Many of the concepts they teach feature in the following pages.

The feature was titled 'What's It Like To Be A PUA?' The acronym stands for 'pick-up artist' - another phrase coined in 'The Game'. I've yet to meet to a dude who dresses in fishnet vests, feather boas and speaks in secret code, like the characters in that book...

You can read the interview at www.thelondondater.co.uk/pua.

3. JUST GO OUT!

Getting better with women is actually no different to becoming a good basketball player. Just practice a lot, learn from your mistakes and improve.

The key difference is that most men won't want to admit they need practice with women. It's seen as a skill we're already supposed to have.

I suppose that's why The LSS was a secret society - and why most of its members would be embarrassed to admit they were part of it.

Still, this was a supportive community. Blokes seen to be 'going out' a lot would be praised. Anyone asking stupid questions would be accused of not 'going out' enough. 'Going out' seemed to be key.

Meeting Adam

The first dude from the forum I met seemed to go out a lot. His name was Adam. He'd clocked up hundreds of posts, including a fair few 'lay reports.'

He suggested we meet at The Book Club in Shoreditch at 21.00. In this part of London, going to the club early is the only way all-male groups are guaranteed to get in. Early starts save you a lot of money in the long run though. Most of the dudes who go out 4-5 nights a week aim to get to the club before it starts charging cover.

Adam could feel the awkwardness emanating off me as we shook hands. Thankfully, he was a fun sociable guy who found it easy meeting strangers.

An absolute boss.

Here was the structure of our sober night out:

Step 1 - Build social momentum: It's common to arrive at the club and not want to socialise with strangers, especially when you're sober. Our brains are naturally resistant to anything uncomfortable. It'll come up with excuse after excuse to keep you in your comfort zone. In order to overcome this, it's best to start building social momentum as soon as you arrive.

That's exactly what we did. We spoke to guys, girls, large groups stood in a circle. Everyone. Essentially, we were showing our brains that it's OK to speak to strangers. Some groups would welcome conversation. Others would find it awkward and excuse themselves. It didn't matter at this stage.

Ideally, you build so much social momentum that you can open a conversation with anyone without thinking twice. This way, when that hot woman appears, you introduce yourself before your brain thinks of an excuse not to.

Building social momentum isn't always easy. Unless you're a massive extrovert, it'll feel awkward and you won't want to do it. Maybe you spent the day in a stressful job, or feel overwhelmed with social anxiety. Perhaps you can't stand getting rejected. I was 'all of the above'.

But as you speak with more people, your self-consciousness will melt away. You'll start opening conversations without thinking. Jokes effortlessly arrive. There are no hidden agendas. There's no hesitation. There's no being unsure of yourself. This is social freedom.

Once you're here, it'll feel like walking on air. Women will open up to you. Your conversation-starters will seem effortlessly smooth. You'll come across as naturally confident. On top of that, you're completely sober, so you're not sloppy, you're not slurring your words and you're still socially aware.

Step 2 - Stick in there: Any man who appears so effortlessly cool will eventually capture a woman's attention, but it'll typically take some time for her to show she's attracted. In fact, she'll probably show disinterest or be a bit mean. You would too if you'd been hit on by thousands of idiots throughout adulthood. This 'bitch shield' is one way she can check you're actually the confident guy you're portraying.

Alternatively, she's acting cold because:

- she doesn't want to appear easy
- she's nervous and doesn't want to say anything silly
- her feet hurt
- she's too drunk
- she's not drunk enough
- millions of other reasons.

It takes time for women to warm up to a man. The average bloke walks away at the first sign of awkwardness. Be that guy who gives it time to blossom.

Often, there'll be awkward silences. She'll show no signs she likes you. She'll insult you! Teach yourself to keep telling stories, making jokes, in spite of this. The better you get at this, the more you'll spot signs she wants you to stay. Now you have something to work with...

(If she really wants to be left alone, she'll tell you or she'll leave. **DON'T** ever stop her from doing that. There's nothing awesome about harassment.)

It takes mental strength to withstand this awkwardness. It's a social muscle you need to build. On that first night at The Book Club, there were many situations I wanted to escape. Women ignoring me. Boyfriends trying to intimidate me. One bloke made fun of my bald head, but I kept having fun and forced myself to stick around for a couple more sentences. As the night went on, it got easier. We had more fun. We felt more social freedom. More females seemed delighted to speak to us.

Step 3 - Pull the trigger: Soon enough, you'll find a woman who's hooked on your every word. She'll laugh at your jokes, respond well to your flirting, ask questions, etc. At this point, it's time to pull the trigger.

As Daniella sat at the table finishing her beer, I opened the conversation with the careless arrogance of a man who had been having fun all night.

"Who are you!?"

Her eyes expanded like a loved-up anime character. She smiled and said she'd just moved to London from Copenhagen. All I could concentrate on was her long blonde hair and skinny legs.

It was closing time and her friend had just jumped in a cab. At the time, all I knew about 'pulling' a woman from a bar to the bedroom was to make a bold decision and hope she'd be down for it. I interrupted her sentence, grabbed her hand and led her out the door.

She asked where we were going.

"Afterparty."

Often, women will throw token objections. This time, it was simple.

We worked out that her flat was the best place for the 'afterparty'. Adam jumped in the taxi too. We kept the laughs and jokes going throughout the journey.

Daniella asked Adam how we knew each other. There's always a moment of panic if the answer to this hasn't been pre-determined.

"TINDER!" he yelled.

She laughed and Adam changed the subject. He'd clearly dealt with this hurdle before. We jumped out of the cab in Stratford. My 'Tinder date' Adam carried on home.

Daniella's flat was the fanciest I'd ever set foot in. She was a banker, and quite clearly a well-paid-one. We sat in the living room with a Spotify playlist and two cans of obscure Danish lager (my first drink of the night).

We spoke about deep topics, such as how soulless it can be working in finance. There was a flirtatious vibe, but no obvious signs she was ready for sex.

I knew that the same principles of 'pulling' apply inside the living room. Be decisive and hope she's down for it. She'll make it clear if she isn't.

As she stepped towards the fridge, I stood up, stopped her and leant in for the kiss. She kissed back passionately, like she'd been waiting for it this whole time. I led her to the bedroom and it quickly escalated to sex. She was happy to take the lead and tell me exactly what she wanted. She purred as I nibbled on her ears and neck. She begged me to take her harder, then screamed as if she'd just paid for the walls to be soundproofed.

It was a wild night. Wealthy ladies aren't always prudes.

Walking past the Olympic Stadium the next morning, my head was spinning. Not from a stinking hangover, but an epiphany. It was now clear I could get really good at seducing women, taking them home and having sex. I wouldn't even need to get pissed, and it worked on sophisticated chicks too.

My second sober one-night stand. If I wasn't hooked after shagging Hannah, I definitely was now.

4. WHAT'S ON THE INSIDE?

How did I do it? From no sex in over a year to sleeping with two gorgeous women in two weeks.

Was it really this 'structure' of a sober night out or these routines I'd read about online? I thought so.

In reality, it was something much simpler.

It was the mood this put me in. The thrill of the chase.

Excitement plus confidence

The 'structure' explained in the previous chapter is fantastic for making you feel socially free. I prefer it to alcohol.

Add the pure excitement emanating from me as a result of moving to London, meeting cool new people, being on reality TV, and it's no wonder everyone wanted to talk to me. Previously, I'd be approaching women desperate for them to become the new Gemma. Now, I was just thrilled to be there. This lack of neediness is so rare that women quickly become attracted to it.

More importantly, I'd discovered an unshakeable confidence. This was partly due to the pick-up lines I'd learned, but mostly in myself. My new employers had chosen me ahead of everyone. The First Dates producers thought I was a legend. Hannah did too, even if only for only for a few hours. Life was looking up again.

Never underestimate the powerful cocktail that is excitement plus confidence. People are excited to listen to excited people. They want to spend more time around them. They won't touch unconfident, unexcited people with a bargepole.

When I started my door-to-door sales career in 2010, I didn't know anything about the product, but I was super-excited to sell it and had seen how easy others had made it look in training. That was all it took to smash my initial targets.

Months later, the initial excitement had worn off and I'd been exposed to failing salesmen. Despite knowing way more theory about sales, I struggled…

Expose yourself to successful people. Copy them, match their enthusiasm, and you'll see similar results. It works in any field.

Being sober in the club

The easiest way to feel excited and confident in the club is to get drunk or take drugs. This triggers the feel-good endorphins in our brain. It shuts off the inner voices that say you're not good enough. Without even thinking, you speak to that pretty girl and it often goes well.

Alcohol has been helping people get laid since the beginning of getting laid. You don't even consider that the woman might not want to be interrupted, that you're not her 'type', that your pick-up line isn't good enough. It has the same effect as 'building social momentum', but involves less effort and is less awkward.

Of course, there is a price to pay. You become sloppy. You don't notice subtle social cues. You don't remember what worked well and what didn't, so you never really improve at speaking to women. The health risks are well documented, as is the ridiculous price of a pint in London. I always found it difficult to stay at peak drunk too. That sweet spot of feeling confident without falling over or drooling on myself was tough to maintain.

That's why I prefer 'building social momentum'. The start of a night out is often awkward, especially when you don't want to speak to anyone. But by the end, you'll be the wittiest and most articulate bloke in the venue.

With experience, you'll start spotting subtle cues in their body language. You see when she's ready to be kissed, when she's pissed off, losing interest, etc. It feels like superpowers.

Alcohol makes you OK with being bored. If there's a song you hate or no-one is really talking, you're still sort of content just standing around. Now, when there's nothing going on, I have to entertain myself. I chat up a cute woman, make a joke with the nearest dude or start a silly dance-off. As a result, sober nights end up epic.

Approach anxiety

The toughest hurdle to jump when you're chatting up women without drinking? Inhibitions.

Without that sweet liquid courage running through your body, it's common to be scared of speaking to sexy women.

Many people fear rejection. Some worry about looking silly in front of other people. Often, it's a fear of getting beaten up by the girl's boyfriend. Humans have supposedly carried these fears since caveman times, when being rejected by the tribe would mean certain death.

This nonsensical sensation has been nicknamed 'approach anxiety'. Here are 8 attitude shifts that can help you overcome it.

Attitude Shift 1 - I'd be a great boyfriend for anyone: Have you ever stopped to think what makes you a brilliant option for a beautiful woman? It's worth doing.

Write down 50 reasons why you're awesome. This exercise is brilliant because it forces your brain to think hard about your positive qualities. You'll rewire your brain to remember your answers, and you'll be armed with 50 reasons why your approach will be welcomed. If you can't complete your list, you should at least be able to identify areas to improve yourself for the future.

Attitude Shift 2 - There's £10,000 in your pocket: If you approached a girl to present her a £10,000 cheque, would you be nervous about her accepting it? Well, if you're cool enough to be able to complete your '50 reasons' list, you're probably presenting a package worth way more than that. Most women would take the man of their dreams over £10,000. A cool, successful, intelligent, loyal partner is probably worth ten times this figure. Always approach with the intention of giving something to the girl, whether it's a laugh, a lasting memory or a taste of your lifestyle. Never be the bloke who takes before he gives.

Attitude Shift 3 - What's the best that can happen? We often see a hot woman and worry about the worst thing that could happen. It's a natural human response that helps us stay away from danger. Yet, we should also weigh up the best thing that could happen. That stranger could be your next sexual partner. Your next girlfriend. She could be the woman you'll marry. Compare the best possible result with the worst. The reward is nearly always worth the risk.

Attitude Shift 4 - It's a man's job to make the approach: Some women spend hours in front of the mirror making themselves look pretty. Meanwhile, it takes you a few seconds to tell her she looks nice.

It's the man's job to speak to the woman and make things happen. Considering how long she spent getting ready, it's almost rude not chatting her up. On the inside, she's praying at least one cool guy has the balls to introduce themselves. So don't slack off! Do your job!

Attitude Shift 5 - It's not rejection. It's lack of chemistry! Humans have a biological urge for affection. It's natural to want to be accepted by everyone. Nevertheless, there are plenty of people that don't have chemistry. Not every girl will like you, and that's OK. Rather than viewing every approach as a pick-up attempt, which can be accepted or rejected, see it as checking whether there's a connection.

Don't be the dude who's desperate to make it work just because she's beautiful. Have higher standards. Explore whether she's right for you in other ways. If she's rude, ignorant or stand-offish, it's not a rejection. There's just no chemistry. You wouldn't want a woman like that anyway, would you?

Attitude Shift 6 - It's a numbers game: If there were 20 gorgeous girls in a bar, and one had a brilliant gift for you, would you feel bad finding out who had it? Or would you excitedly approach each and every one until you got your gift? Once you received your gift, would you think twice about the girls who didn't have it? It's a silly idea, but not too different from real life! Approach gorgeous girls with a great attitude intact and I'd imagine more than 5% will be willing to give you something.

Attitude Shift 7 - I'm not special (in a stranger's eyes): No-one cares about a stranger's actions if it doesn't affect them. You're not that special. See for yourself by screaming at the top of your lungs in a public place. People will stare for two seconds, then turn back around. They're too preoccupied with their own lives. Realise this and you'll have no reason to worry about other people's opinions.

Also, if a woman shoos you away, it's because you're a stranger. Don't take it personally. After all, she doesn't even know you personally.

Attitude Shift 8. It feels better than not doing it: Here's what's worse than getting rejected by a woman: that gut-twisting feeling of 'what if?' Was she supposed to be my next sexual adventure, my next girlfriend? Once I've introduced myself, I never beat myself up about anything else, and neither should you. See every approach as a ten out of ten from thereon. You'll either win her over or you'll learn and do better next time. The only way you lose is by not doing it.

What to say to a girl

These attitude shifts might make sense, but what if you can't think of the right thing to say?

Back in the day, I'd rely heavily on the pick-up lines written in these online articles.

There are basic principles about what works well. For example, girls often respond to lines that hint about how they're perceived.

"You know what they say about women who X?"
"There's something about you that makes me think Y."

Lines which incorporate the whole group also work well.

"You guys look like you're some sort of Z."

These worked well, but not because they're fascinating conversation starters. It was because I believed in them so strongly.

I'd seen these lines captivate so many women that I'd step up knowing they'd want to hear them. It's so simple to capture someone's attention when you truly believe in what you're saying.

Eventually, I had this epiphany: you can say whatever you want.

I've picked up girls using preposterous 'chat-up lines':

"Can you buy me a glass of water?"
"My name has two Es in it!"
"Do you like my shirt? It's ironed."

When the club is really loud, I wave my arm and shout *"HELLO."*

Ridiculous. Stupid. Still, these lines all worked for the same reason. They've also all not worked for the exact same reason. Sub-communications.

Scientists claim that 93% of communication is non-verbal. This means your sub-communications are thirteen times more important than your actual chat.

Confident body language is crucial. Eye contact is essential. But here's the most important factor: belief that whatever comes out of your mouth is brilliant. As narcissistic as it sounds, you need to believe your gob is an unrelenting goldmine of hilarity and fascination.

Have you ever been around a bunch of blokes having such a brilliant time that you can't help but be in a better mood? Or spoke to someone so passionate about a subject that you find yourself forming an interest too? It's as if their emotions (amusement, passion, happiness) are being transferred onto you. Psychologists call this the law of state transference – and it actually works. Whatever you find funny, others will find funny. Even shitty stories of how you ironed your own shirt. The sting is you really need to believe it. You need an unshakeable belief that your stories are the nuts.

How to always have something to say

There's something sexy about the person who can speak with no filter. They're unstifled. They're unpredictable. They're assured. It's such an attractive trait.

It's also a social muscle you can train. Get in the habit of approaching hotties without having anything in your head. As quickly as possible, say 'excuse me', then see what else comes out.

They might not react right away. Maybe they're shy, they misheard or they're in a bad mood, so be prepared to do most of the talking for the first minute or so. Anything you find funny or interesting should eventually help her open up. The more you notice this, the easier it becomes to believe you have that million-pound mouthpiece. This technique makes flirting more fun. You're sharing what you find funny, rather than trying to win someone over. Women will usually enjoy it more too. It's more entertaining than the traditional conversations they're used to.

There's only one reason you'd struggle to think of anything: your standards for what's good enough to say. They're set too high. Don't put women on this pedestal. Anything that's amusing or interesting to you will usually be so to them. Make sure you throw in some flirting too. Self-amusement will capture her attention, but you can't be a dancing clown for the whole conversation.

Crucial: this technique won't work when you're not carefree. Before I understood this, I remember spotting this breathtaking woman and racking my brain for the best thing to say.

'How about the one with the ironed shirt? That worked the weekend before!'

Not this time. The tone was off. The delivery was awkward. I was using it to impress her, rather than to amuse myself. She physically cringed and walked away without saying anything. Yesterday's worldie-winning banter becomes tomorrow's crutch when it's coming from the wrong place.

The power of rejection

Rejection is inevitable when you're meeting women this way, and as you're sober you'll remember the harshest ones.

"Mate, you look like Voldemort!"
"Eurgh, how fucking old are you!?"
"What the fuck, you look like my dad!?"

The advantage of taking these rejections square in the face is that you become an icy mother-fucker.

Take enough of them and you'll no longer approach women fearing rejections. You've survived enough of them to realise what doesn't kill you makes you stronger - the type of guy who stays grounded regardless of what women throw at him.

Eventually, you'll be able to go through a whole night of bullshit and still be confident enough to pull that stunner at closing time. That's a great feeling by the way... You almost wish all the mean girls you met could watch you shagging that hottie who's way prettier than them.

As explained before, it shouldn't hurt that badly. These girls aren't rejecting you, because they barely know you. What's worse is when a girl initially likes you, spends half the night getting to know you, then goes home alone. Or even with someone else!

That's when you can feel your chest hurting, because it's based on something you did wrong. Maybe you let some other dude steal her away. Perhaps you creeped her out on the way home.

Whatever happened, I'd encourage you to stew in that pain. Write down what went wrong. Put yourself through it again, because that suffering ensures you learn from your mistake. A bit like a child scolding his hand on the stove.

These experiences will frustrate you. They'll break your heart, but ultimately turn you into the person who plows through any obstacle to get the job done.

You'll stop fearing rejection in other areas of life too. Maybe you'll finally ask for that raise or put out that creative project you were scared of sharing.

The coolest men in the world have been through the toughest hardships. The most talented have failed the most times. So, start seeing rejections as something you need to truly slay it with women.

Forget about being 'out of her league'

I'm far from any girl's 'type' physically. I'm 5'9", bald with facial scars and crow's feet, but I've never considered myself out of anyone's league since following this process.

If you're approaching properly, you're in the Premier League: Let's say you spot the girl of your dreams. It could be at the bar early in the evening when no-one is wasted. Maybe she's shopping for groceries or strolling through the park. The majority of men won't even introduce themselves in these situations.

Even in more acceptable environments, most who do say hi to her are half-expecting rejection. They speak without conviction. They say stupid things and give up at the first sign of awkwardness. Just by stepping up with strong eye contact, a clear voice and some self-belief, you're putting yourself among the most eligible men.

Looks don't matter: Yes, appearance plays a part in winning her over. By all means, work on your fashion and join the gym. Women prefer a handsome man over a haggard mess, but here's what matters more:

- you're awesome fun to be around
- you have a good sense of humour and social skills
- you're adventurous, passionate, interesting, etc.
- you understand the basics of flirting
- you're an alpha male who believes in himself.

Here's a scientifically-proven peculiarity about human perception. This masculine behaviour will actually trick her brain into thinking you're more handsome than you are.

Have you browsed through photos of an ex and wondered what you were thinking, even though you used to be besotted? Or seen yourself in the mirror and cringed, despite being delighted with your appearance days earlier? If so, you're experiencing the brain's reticular activating system (RAS) in action. It controls our selective focus, deciding what captures our attention and what remains a background blur.

This function is programmed to focus on whatever matches our inner belief system. If we believe someone is seriously awesome, our RAS searches for evidence to back that up. When we don't like someone, our brain focuses on their flaws. This works for both personalities and physical features. Yes, our brains actually perceive other people's appearances differently depending on how we feel about them.

Go out and see for yourself.

5. FROM BAR TO BEDROOM

So, we've learned how to become socially free and believe in our own awesomeness.

This is CRUCIAL to getting the hottest girls. It's more important than looks, money or any pick-up lines you can learn.

However, there are some skills that'll make it much easier to get that girl from bar to bedroom within hours of meeting her.

How to talk forever

For men, attraction is like a light switch. They see a hot woman and they're instantly ready for sex.

Women work differently. It takes them longer to get comfortable with you, so you'll need to put the time in conversationally.

A lot of men struggle to talk endlessly. They find it tough to maintain a woman's attention, especially in an environment where there's loud music, drunk friends, superstar DJs, other single dudes, etc.

Fortunately, being a fascinating conversationalist is something you can learn. Here are 7 tips to help you talk forever.

1. No filters: Already mentioned, but worth repeating as it's the number one tip for talking forever.

The main reason we can't open or continue conversations is because we're worried what we have to say isn't good enough. Notice how you're never short of things to say to your best friend, because you're not desperately trying to impress them. Adopt this attitude with women too. It'll not only open up your mind, but it'll also help you appear more attractive.

Don't be afraid to be outrageous either. Make that risqué joke, start that bizarre conversation, tease her, just like you would with your mates. Light-hearted teasing shows we're comfortable with someone, which in turn makes them comfortable with us.

Most men play it safe in their conversations because they're scared to mess things up, so this will help you stand out. If you overstep the mark, tone it back and speak about something more relatable.

Remember, 93% of communication is non-verbal anyway. Women are ultimately more interested in the vibe behind what you're saying than the content.

2. Use assumptions, not questions: Ask too many questions and your flirting will feel more like an interview. Guess where she's from or what she does for a living, rather than asking her. This is more fun, playful and interesting. She'll probably ask why you made such an assumption. All of a sudden she's invested in the conversation…

3. Use time travel: If the topic of your conversation is grounded in the present moment, you're seconds away from it grinding to a halt. Move the conversation into the past or the future, and it should develop nicely.

Let's say you're talking about coffee. If you comment on the taste of the coffee, she'll probably offer her opinion and that's that. However, you could continue the conversation by telling a story about the best/worst coffee you ever tasted (past). Similarly, you could ask if she ever fancied opening her own coffee shop (future).

4. Screen: Think of three qualities you're looking for in a woman and find out if she has them. Now, you've got three fresh conversation topics at your fingertips.

Women want to earn a cool guy's attention. It's a turn-off if they feel you're instantly won over. Screening is a brilliant method of framing yourself as the chooser, rather than the chaser.

Remember, assumptions not questions.

"You look like you're sporty/a party animal/adventurous, etc."

(These are my three).

5. Determine logistics: Find out where she lives, who she's with and what she's doing the next day. This information can spark interesting conversations. More importantly, you can use it to determine whether to shoot for a one-night stand or a date in the future.

6. Open your eyes and ears: Rather than being stuck in your thoughts desperately searching for conversation topics, discuss the environment around you. In a bar or a club, there'll always be the song that's playing, the drinks they're serving, the dodgy dancing, etc.

Even better, say something you notice about her. Maybe she's wearing some strange jewellery or has a cute giggle...

Also, LISTEN. It's the simplest tip of all, but one that most men struggle with. Rather than lining up your next story, open your ears. She'll almost definitely offer up a topic you can latch on to.

7. Flirt: As pleasant as it is to come across as an incredible conversationalist, it'll count for nothing if you don't show your intentions. Throw in compliments, some light playful touches. Take her to the dance floor. These are the moments she'll remember. Yes, you're risking ruining a pleasant conversation by escalating this way. Still, failing to do it earns you a one-way ticket to the friendzone.

Being an incredible conversationalist will benefit you in other areas of life. You'll find it easier to make friends. You'll stand out in job interviews. You'll be better at any pursuit that involves talking.

In London, the rental market is so overcrowded you often have to 'audition' for a room to let. Typically, the current tenants invite a ton of applicants to meet them, then pick the one they like best to live with them.

The last time I did this, I stayed ten minutes longer than everyone else and befriended the woman showing us around her shared house in Tooting. She was a hot, skinny 21-year-old. Before stumbling across the advice in this book, I'd have felt awkward and left with the rest of the applicants. Sticking around is one of the best decisions I've ever made. I got the room and the other tenants ended up becoming my best friends.

Overcoming shit tests

Here's an epiphany that blew my mind. When hot girls are mean to you, it's often because they're attracted.

Yes, sometimes they seriously want you to leave them alone. Perhaps because you've offended them, come at them with a creepy vibe or shown a clear lack of confidence. Often here, they'll promptly tell you to fuck right off or just walk away, and who can blame them? How polite and tolerant are you when a homeless person asks for spare change? What if dozens of bums approached you every time you went out to party?

This is the reality for hot women. Most men who approach them are drunk, creepy, weird, etc. As such, they develop this autopilot defence mechanism whenever any dude approaches. Accept you're also a creepy, drunk criminal in her mind until you prove otherwise.

In these first few minutes of meeting a woman, expect her to be cold, distant, even rude. This is partly because you're a stranger and she's still unsure about you. Guys with no confidence typically give up within these first few minutes of disinterest. It's your job to remain fun, flirty and confident in spite of this.

It might take her a while to open up. In fact, as you get further into the conversation, it's common she'll start pointing out your deepest insecurities. This is nonsensical and incredibly mean. But if she does this, it's almost definitely because SHE LIKES YOU.

These insults are also known as 'shit tests'. She's testing to see if you're actually the confident guy you're portraying yourself as. Be pleased when you come across a shit test. She wouldn't bother testing someone she has no interest in. If she really disliked you, she'd just leave.

It could take a few hours of teasing and banter before she believes you're the real deal, so you better embrace the fact you're short, lanky, bald, black, white, hairy, fat, skinny, old, young, etc.

Plenty of girls I've slept with laughed at me for being short and bald. Ironically, most don't actually care if a guy has these supposed physical disadvantages; they just need to know that YOU don't care either. They're scanning for insecurities. Don't show them.

This won't happen every time a woman is attracted. Some will happily stand and chat; others will become timid and shy, but it's important to be prepared if these bitchy tests come flying at you.

Let's look at some ways to pass the classic shit test:

"You are too old for me."

1. Agree and amplify: *"Yeah, I could be your father. Call me Daddy."*

2. Misinterpret as a compliment: *"Thanks, but don't worry. You don't seem that immature."*

3. Misinterpret as flirting: *"It must be intimidating speaking to a man with such wisdom and experience."*

4. Dismiss and change the subject: *"Sure, the drinks are super-cheap here, right?"*

5. Anything that shows you don't care: *"Yep, I'm also short and bald."*

Don't flinch and swiftly change the subject after you've passed the test.

If you want to fail a shit test, defend yourself. Ideally, use logic.

"Actually, there's only ten years between us. My parents have a twelve-year age gap."

Cool story, bro. Sayonara.

How to pull

The logistics of a one-night stand are as crucial as being attractive. If you're in the centre of big cities like London, it's likely the girl either lives hours away or is a tourist.

Even if she's fallen madly in love with you, good luck convincing her to share a half-hour cab journey to the deepest depths of South London.

Add in the fact that she'll almost always be there with friends, won't want to look like a slut, will have things to do in the morning...Suddenly, getting a one-night stand seems tougher than smuggling drugs into Colombia. Here are some tips to help get around these obstacles.

Screen logistics:

"Where do you live?"
"Who are you here with?"
"What are you doing tomorrow?"

Sprinkling these questions into the conversation early on will save you hours of hassle. If you are after a one-night stand, a girl who needs to travel back to the outskirts of Essex might not be the one for you. You can still grab her contact details, but only if that first date is worth two hours on the Central line.

Baby-step: Women love sex just as much as men. Sadly, they carry this societal pressure not to give themselves away as easily.

That's why "want to come back to mine and fuck" won't work, even if she's secretly fantasising about a night of passion with you. They don't want to be seen as filthy sluts. They need to be able to justify to their friends and themselves that 'it just happened'. It's up to you to play this game.

Rather than ask her directly to your bedroom, baby-step her somewhere it's easier to agree to.

First, find a reason to step outside. Then, perhaps grab some food. Maybe find a fun venue closer to your home. Finally, an excuse to go back to the house. It could be an afterparty. It could be more drinks or watching a film. Any excuse that isn't sex works just fine.

Women know what's up. It's a little white lie which both parties are in on. Any suggestion that baby-stepping is 'tricking women into bed' is an insult to their intelligence. They just need that excuse to rationalise that 'it just happened'.

Once you get home, take your time. Don't put too much pressure on her. If she's come this far, sex will often be on the cards. After all, sex is awesome and we all want it. Sadly, it's still taboo for women to admit this.

Dealing with drama and obstacles: There'll almost be some sort of obstacle or drama that makes this more difficult than it needs to be. These obstacles help create epic stories. Embrace them, then overcome them. It's the epic stories you remember decades later, not the easy one-night stands.

Here's an example of the bullshit you'll have to go through.

- Spot sexy blonde student on the dance floor
- Barge through huge crowd of loser tourists
- Yell over woeful reggae/grime track to get her attention
- Befriend all her friends to prevent them cockblocking
- Pepper in stories about this 'amazing fish and chips shop' around the corner
- She insists she's not hungry
- Keep her entertained until she's hungry
- Deal with drunk idiots hitting on her
- Drag her out of the club to buy fish and chips
- Suggest visiting this 'brilliant shisha bar' by my house
- She's left her bag and coat in the club though...
- Walk back to the club, but the bouncer won't let us back in
- Phone her drunk mates and get them to come outside
- Ask her drunk mates to vouch for us
- Queue at the cloakroom
- More drunk idiots and loser tourists hitting on her...
- Walk back to the bus stop with her bag and coat
- Keep her entertained on the bus
- Explain how Tooting isn't that from her house
- Arrive at the 'brilliant shisha bar', which is closed
- Feign disappointment
- Stroll back to my house for 'drinks' instead
- Wait for her to finish phone calls from her worried friends
- Think of a fun thing to show her in my bedroom
- Kiss her (for the first time that evening)
- Escalate from there.

This shit is par for the course for one-night stands. It didn't even make the cut for the 'epic sex stories' chapter at the end of this book. If you usually experience less drama than this, it's because you're only getting the girls that make it easy.

Bear in mind that most girls are trying to walk in high heels after a few drinks. They're still throwing shit tests at you including 'OK, but we're not going any further' at every step of the journey.

It's not always glamorous pulling girls home from nightclubs, and you'll lose a lot of them on the way. Still, the epic sex stories are almost always worth it.

6. DAYGAME

The best thing about learning to hit on women while sober is that you can do it anywhere. On the street, in the shopping centre, wherever you see them.

Let's rewind to the Saturday Sarge. My first ever attempt at this:

The January drizzle was threatening to turn to full-on rain. Surely, no woman would stop to talk to us in this miserable weather? I still remember the exact advice that Jake, our glossy blonde Jesus of a coach, gave us.

- Let the woman walk past, turn, catch up and step in front of her. (This move has a name: 'The Yad Stop').

- Start with a statement of empathy, then a statement of intent. Mine was: "Hi, I know this is a bit random, but I spotted you and thought you looked really nice, so I wanted to meet you". ('Nice' works well because it's a compliment, but it's not too forward).

- Make an assumption about her personality. (This sparks more curiosity than a question. She'll usually ask why you made that assumption. Now you're in a conversation.)

This structure is known as the 'London Daygame Model'. Jake would point out women, slyly listen in and give us feedback after we were done. The others were all nervous to try it. I remember being intrigued, but unconvinced it would work.

The 'approach anxiety' was apparent in all of us. Jake introduced us to some social freedom exercises to help with this. He made us clap our hands above our head, then sing a Britney Spears song at the top of our lungs.

In both of these instances, we soon noticed no-one gave a shit what we were doing. No-one ever gives a shit about strangers on the street. They'll look at you for a few seconds before going back to their stupid inner thoughts. Once you've 'embarrassed' yourself in public like we did, it'll be seem comparatively sensible and therefore easier to chat up a woman.

I approached three or four women that afternoon. No phone numbers, but they all stopped to talk for a short while before excusing themselves. That was enough to convince me that Jake could turn water into wine.

Social momentum works in the daytime too, so it's best to practice daygame where there's a high volume of people. It's no good not strolling around for hours without a hot woman to speak to. Crowded places also provide anonymity, which can be advantageous if you're not very good at it yet.

Oxford Street in London is known as one of the best daygame spots in the world. It's by far the most popular location to practice. Once you're aware of this, you'll probably spot a daygamer. Women in need of an ego boost need only stroll the length of this shopping street. They'll probably be approached and complimented by a ballsy guy. Covent Garden, Camden, Leicester Square and Westfield Shopping Centres are popular spots too.

Daygame and 'approach anxiety'

Speaking to strangers in bars and clubs is more socially acceptable, compared to the street. Because of this, many people find it tougher to approach a beautiful woman during the day. Massive respect to anyone with the balls to do it.

The first time I tried it without a wingman went atrociously. I wandered the streets of Leicester Square for 59 minutes convincing myself to say something, anything! Excuses came from everywhere. She's walking too fast, she's wearing headphones, she seems busy etc.

Eventually, I stopped a woman and blurted out something about her shoes. My voice trembled with terror. She said thanks and immediately excused herself. The most cringeworthy interaction ever, but I was so chuffed with myself. The tension dissipated from my neck and shoulders. Is that all I was worried about?

I soon learned daygame is similar to skydiving, public speaking or anything else you might be afraid of.

- The longer you stand there, the tougher it is to dive in.

- The fear disappears once you're actually doing it.

- Afterwards, you feel exhilarated and really proud of yourself.

- The more you do it, the more numb you become to the fear. You'll eventually learn to love the adrenaline rush.

The magic of daygame

On my second Saturday Sarge, I exchanged numbers with an underwear model - a tanned brunette sporting a summer dress and designer sunglasses. She was stood outside Debenhams with her dad.

An intimidating situation. Some might think it's a seemingly impossible one. Surely, it takes more than 'I thought you looked really nice' to win this woman over?

Not really.

I was in a brilliant mood having built up social momentum. I approached with a big smile, strong eye contact, tons of cheerful energy, yet not particularly caring how it turned out. That's an emotional cocktail with one hell of a kick.

There are not many dudes who could chat her up in the middle of the day with such confidence. Even if you're short, bald, etc., you'll stand out. Because who else has the balls to do this? This is the magic of daygame.

I only dabbled with daygame for the first couple of years, but I could see why some guys found it so addictive. There's something beautiful about breaking the boredom of everyday life to compliment a stranger. Sure, some girls are in a hurry, some aren't in the mood to socialise, but many women told me it made their day. It still gives me butterflies every time I try it, but I'm a strong believer of doing something that scares you every day. There's not a daytime approach I regret doing.

What's more, there's no terrible music to shout over, less distractions, fewer friends dragging her to the toilet. You can really clean up on the streets...

There's something so brilliantly unpredictable about daygame. I've been on some incredible 'instant-dates' (heading somewhere immediately after meeting her) with stunning women and stayed in touch afterwards.

This includes a 19-year-old Swedish literature student, a successful author and a self-improvement business owner. None of these women liked going to nightclubs, and if they were on Tinder you can bet they'd be bombarded with messages. Still, if you're a daygamer, you're not competing with the dudes on her smartphone. You've got the balls to introduce yourself in real life.

The worst date I ever had (but the best story) started when I chatted up a Swedish woman at a bus stop. Don't worry, that's included in the epic sex stories chapter.

Before you skip to that, subscribe to the YouTube channels of 'Street Attraction' and 'Daygame.com'

These are the best daygame coaches based in London, and their channels brilliantly demonstrate how far you can take it.

7. DATING MADE EASY

Dating tends to be more difficult in big cities. There are studies that prove that. London might be one of the toughest cities to find a partner. After all:

We're too busy: Londoners are commitment-phobes. With extra hours in the office (or last-minute cocktails with work colleagues) so common, we'd do well to commit to a dinner date, let alone a relationship. Why arrange a potentially awkward first date when there's so much else to see and do? If we're not too busy, we're too exhausted from our ten-hour working day and two-hour commute.

There's too much choice: There's seven million Londoners. We simply have too many potential partners to pick from, especially since the emergence of Tinder and other online dating applications. Why settle for anyone when there are thousands of alternatives just a right swipe away?

There's too much distance: If you meet someone sexy in the city centre, it's likely they live ten miles or more away. Our capital city is too sparse, and no-one is fit enough to make that two-hour tube journey worth it.

We're too unfriendly: A lot of Londoners are in too much of a hurry to stop for smalltalk. With crime rates so high, we're terrified when a stranger even smiles at us. Ultimately, this makes many of us less open to the possibility of a romantic encounter in public.

That's why exchanging phone numbers can be so frustrating. The woman might have adored you at the time, but these excuses not to meet you are easy to give in to.

Still, there are actions that'll turn the tables in your favour.

How to ask a girl out

Spend as much time with her as possible: Many men make the mistake of taking her number, then running away before they mess things up. The more time she spends with you, the surer she can be that you're worth taking out on a date. That's why the 'instant-date' is so powerful.

Even if you haven't got enough time for this, you've hopefully at least discussed something you can do together. Ideally, you've also discovered when she's free to do it.

This way, your first message only needs to confirm these plans, and you don't have to go through the painful process of organising all this through text.

No questions in text messages: Never open conversations with questions. Constructing an answer to 'How was your weekend?' will never top her priorities if she's still not sure about you.

It might seem counterproductive, but it's a better strategy to text her a funny or interesting nugget from your day. She'll reply if she wants to, but there's no pressure on her. If she doesn't reply, it's not a 'rejection' per se because you've not asked for one.

For this reason, you can send multiple ping texts without coming across as needy. Often, girls won't reply to my first text. Maybe they were in a bad mood. Maybe it got lost in the backlog of other thirsty dudes. Whatever... Fire a few of these funny nuggets at her without asking for anything in return, and they'll often respond.

If you're trying to find something out, make assumptions and let her correct them.

Keep it simple: Firstly, don't text your life story. Most of your texts should lead towards arranging the date. You can be funny, charming and charismatic in person.

Secondly, keep your date ideas simple. Overly thoughtful and brilliant date ideas put too much pressure on the woman.

Stick with drinks in a fun cafe or cocktail bar. A barbeque in a field. Anything she can easily agree to, knowing she can get out quickly if she feels uncomfortable. It's your personality that'll impress her, not the date idea.

Ideally, it's somewhere near your house or hers. Heading back to the bedroom should be as simple as possible. There's nothing like a lengthy tube journey to put out the flames of passion.

A normal date with mind-blowing sex will be more memorable than any quirky date idea.

(Yes, I organise an email newsletter that suggests 7 unique, fun London date ideas every Monday. Subscribe at www.thelondondater.co.uk/dates. These tips are more suitable for couples though.)

Act fast: A week is a long time in the world of a gorgeous woman. It's likely she's been hit on a fair few times and received hundreds of Tinder matches. Don't wait a few days to text her. Organise that date while she still remembers how awesome you are.

How to behave on a date

If a woman meets you for a date in spite of all these excuses not to be there, she definitely likes you. So RELAX.

Treating first dates like a big deal puts too much pressure on the woman, and that leaves no room for her to feel attraction.

Sex on a first date should feel like saving par in golf. You've taken a little longer than necessary, but all the obstacles are out of the way. Ideally, you're really close to the hole. Just finish the job.

Enjoy her company, treat her as if she already adores you, find an excuse to head back to your place. It should be easy. Far easier than dragging her off a crowded dance floor in front of all her mates anyway. Sure, she may still throw some shit tests at you, but we know how to pass these now.

Why seal the deal so quickly?

By all means, treat a woman to tons of fantastic dates before trying to sleep with her. Maybe you're the type of guy who wants to build a great connection before getting intimate. It's up to you...In my experience, great sex is the best way to make a girl want to see you again. Orgasms are a powerful incentive.

Women aren't always looking for a provider-male to become their boyfriend. Sometimes, they're in a stage where they're only after wild no-strings sex. Why not give her that first, then see where it leads?

Tinder and online dating

Tinder and its copycat apps have taken the dating world by storm. It would be wrong not to mention them. They're a great tool for traditionally good-looking people to find dates and even relationships.

Still, this book is about how to stand out from the masses. Tinder is the antithesis of this.

It essentially eliminates all the skills mentioned so far in this book. You're on a level playing field with people who wouldn't ever be brave enough to talk to women in real life. If you're a bald 29-year-old with crow's feet, it's less than a level playing field. You're left with low-quality leads at best.

Staring at a smartphone and swiping is not my idea of fun. It's not been efficient for me - and there's less of a guarantee you'll actually get on with the girls who want to meet you. There's no thrill of the chase going on here...

I pulled a beautiful blonde dancer from Be At One recently and spotted she had over 1,000 Plenty of Fish notifications on her iPhone. ONE THOUSAND. There really are plenty of fish trying to get laid online. If you get in front of her face on a Friday night, you can outcompete all of them.

Having said that, I have been on two Tinder dates and one went exceptionally well, as you'll see in the next chapter.

8. HOW TO GET AN INCREDIBLE GIRLFRIEND

Once I was immersed in singledom, the idea of settling into a relationship was borderline disgusting.

The thought of cosy nights on the sofa bored me to tears. The memories of Sunday afternoons with a girlfriend's parents were cringeworthy. The bickering and compromises that come with relationships did not appeal at all. I had seductive superpowers now. I was hooked on testing and strengthening them.

I'd hit the clubs every other day and practice daygame in between. These adventures were satisfying my urge to live each day like my last. It felt empowering wondering what women I'd meet, be it on the streets or in a bar. I'd soldier through my office job sleep-deprived because I'd spent Tuesday night shagging some university student. My dirty little secret.

As I sat waiting to meet a new wingman, I'd picture my 'normal' friends settling down to watch Game of Thrones or something similarly monotonous. Counting down the days to the weekend. That wasn't the lifestyle for me.

This wasn't just about the thrill of seeing a new woman naked. It was also this addictive sensation of social freedom, partying and meeting pretty girls. I'd sacrifice the passion and stability of a steady relationship forever to keep feeling this. To get the best girls, you have to put yourself in that amazing mood. I got really good at doing that. On the best nights, my wingmen and I would have more fun than anyone else in the club, and the girls would gravitate towards us.

Even on the terrible nights where no-one wanted to talk to us, we'd learn a ton. If I could become good enough at this to get a steady flow of one-night stands, I felt I would do it forever. I was in love with singledom.

The best attitude for a relationship

Ironically, that's a crucial attitude for finding an amazing girlfriend. Women don't want a man who melts at their feet as soon as they meet, like I would do after losing Gemma.

Masculine energy desires freedom. Men are programmed to spread their seed as widely as possible. It's inherently unmasculine to be desperate for a single woman.

That's why women are repelled by needy men. They want a man they have to fight for. They want to be chosen as the best option from many.

This isn't what Hollywood tells us. In films and TV shows, the protagonist typically becomes obsessed with a particular woman. He pursues her relentlessly, often at the expense of other things in his life. He 'falls' in love with her, she eventually succumbs to his advances, and they live happily ever after.

That's not how it works in real life.

I've 'fallen' for three women, but none of them were particularly special. At that time I would have fallen for any pretty girl who showed some interest. When we 'fall' in love with someone, our brains inflate their better features and block out their flaws, because we're so desperate to continue receiving their affection. The needy, desperate behaviour that results will scare most emotionally healthy women away. However, it will attract other women with low self-esteem and a lack of suitable options. Two people 'falling' in love with each other. It's called co-dependency.

The cracks in co-dependent pairings appear pretty quickly. They're fraught with jealousy, paranoia and, attempts to limit each other's freedom. The stress of having to handle their partner's insecurities as well as their own. Still, neither party will leave because they're terrified of losing the love and attention they're addicted to. In spite of the stress, it's typically their only source of true happiness.

'Jumping' in love

A high-value man doesn't 'fall' in love. He jumps in. He already has great hobbies and great friends, so he's not desperate for attention from women.

This doesn't mean he's incapable of loving the right lady. He'll give plenty of them a slice of his rollercoaster lifestyle. Then, when he meets a woman that makes his life even better, he'll make an unclouded choice to invest in her. It's a CHOICE rather than an overwhelming urge.

It sounds unromantic, but it's also really unselfish. He doesn't need her to be happy. She isn't this perfect Disney princess that will complete him. Because he's been with enough women before committing, he can clearly see which one has the strengths for a sensational relationship.

It's a logical choice, not an emotional one. That's what happens when you hold yourself from falling in love with the first woman who will have you. This patient approach has the best probability of creating a perfect partnership.

Meeting Olivia

I met Olivia through Tinder. This was nine months after moving to London when the app was still the next big thing. Given everything I'd learned since moving there, meeting her through this 'mainstream' method felt like a badge of shame.

As soon as we sat down to eat, she started dropping some classic shit tests.

"My housemate swiped right on you for banter."
"You're shorter than I imagined."
her phone buzzes *"My housemates say you sound like a wanker."*

Luckily, I'd learned that shit tests mean she likes you. I laughed these off like they didn't even happen.

After our burgers, I baby-stepped her to a pub closer to her house.

"I know this amazing pub."

Then to her front door.

"I'll walk you home like a gentleman."

Then inside.

"Can I use your bathroom real quick?"

Then to her bedroom.

"Show me your taxidermy."

A steamy make-out session followed, but no sex. It actually took four dates to sleep with her, but I didn't mind because she was actually fun to spend time with.

She had a bunch of quirky hobbies and was bang into her fitness. She was funny, full of happiness, and looked way younger than her 28 years.

She thinks I'd never have called her if we'd slept together on that first date. That couldn't be further from the truth.

If a woman is funny, interesting and sexy, she's getting a call back after the first date. If she ALSO shows she's good in bed, a dude would be crazy not to see her again! Sex is the best way to build an emotional connection and to keep a guy thinking about you. When it finally happened, I was hooked.

The right girl at the right time

Here's the key point: it wouldn't have worked out if we'd matched a few months earlier.

At that point, something would have signalled that I didn't deserve her.

She'd have seen it in my body language. I'd have buckled at her shit tests. I'd have been too scared to baby-step her home. I'd have texted her too often or said needy things in my messages.

These subtleties were why I'd never dated anyone successfully since Gemma. Women are so attuned to them.

However, now I was already dating other women. Plus, I found meeting them more fun than the prospect of having a girlfriend. This allowed me to be carefree in all my communications with Olivia.

It opens the brain to speak without filters. It stops you worrying about impressing anyone. It makes you delighted with life regardless of how the date goes. This mood is what women are describing when they tell guys to 'just be themselves.'

Soon enough though, it became obvious that these other women couldn't hold a candle to Olivia.

I was super-resistant to becoming exclusive with her. That would mean giving up this hobby I'd become hooked on. I wasn't ready.

It wasn't sex with new women I'd miss most. I loved the freedom of flirting with anyone and being the most charismatic man in the club. I could see how this was making me more confident in other areas of life. Even so, I eventually became sick of meeting women who were nowhere near as fun and sexy as Olivia.

The exact moment I decided to make her my girlfriend? A Tuesday night on the Tube - heading to some student party in Soho. I'd rushed out of Olivia's house so I wouldn't be late for my introverted Asian wingman, but she was all I could think about. It'd break my heart if she was out doing the same thing. I texted my wingman some excuse about an emergency and went exclusive with Olivia the next day.

Before you ask anyone to be your girlfriend, wait until it's borderline insane not to. Become so awesome at being single that even at this stage you try to fight it. That's how you know you've got a girl that's a great match for you - and you haven't just settled.

It's naturally masculine to resist being tied down. Masculine energy is constantly seeking to escape constraints. Women should always be asking 'so what are we?' first.

Olivia had been single for five years. She said she'd had plenty of interest from men, but they were all 'too desperate to be her boyfriend'. They'd 'smothered her' and didn't allow her to do her own thing.

Can't keep me out the club

I was still at the club three or four nights a week. Going out with my wingmen was still way more fun than clubbing with my normal friends. None of those guys were up for a Wednesday night out anyway.

I'd still flirt with women, just without kissing or taking phone numbers. Once they were interested, I'd palm them off to my mates. This lack of neediness made me even more magnetic. Women would throw themselves at me. They're drawn to anyone offering pure fun with no agenda.

I was never tempted to cheat on Olivia though. Cheating is for people so insecure that love from their partner isn't enough to validate them. It's also for people too scared to leave an unhappy relationship. I don't see why anyone who 'jumped' in love would cheat.

Either way, it was getting easier to hook the hottest girl's attention. A higher percentage of women were reacting well to me. Spotting yourself improving at something is incredibly addictive, especially when the potential reward is mind-blowing sex.

Why *all* men should regularly flirt with women

There are two main reasons all men should go out and flirt with women, even if they have a girlfriend.

For one, it keeps you sharp. Approaching strangers becomes abnormal and scary again if you've not done it in a while. No-one wants to start from the 'scared little bitch' stage once they're back on the singles market.

More importantly, though, it keeps your relationship from going stale.

Humans will naturally conserve energy whenever they can. They'll only put effort into something if there's significant reason to do so. That's why women will initially blow your mind sexually, only for the freaky-naughty action to fade away once they have you.

I don't blame them. Women have all sorts of hormonal changes affecting their sexual appetite. If a stressed, exhausted hormonal woman senses her man will stay either way, she won't exert that extra effort in the bedroom.

Olivia was her best self throughout the entire relationship. I would tell her how brilliant she was all the time, but she could sense I'd walk the second she wasn't the best possible option for me. I'd tell her to do the same if I wasn't the best boyfriend. A woman like her could walk into a new relationship within seconds if she wanted…

This attitude might sound exhausting, or even cruel, but it resulted in an explosive relationship. We'd re-seduce each other every day. We kept putting in the effort to make each other smile. We'd go on unique, imaginative dates. The sex remained raunchy, loving and passionate, even years later.

I jumped in love, and it felt like a never-ending tandem skydive.

9. HOW TO GET OVER HEARTBREAK

Once you start to share meaningful experiences, meet her friends and family, go through high and lows, this skydive transitions into the unconditional love you'd have for a family member.

Olivia was so fun to hang out with and I loved making her happy. When I was with her, I'd enjoy household chores, Sunday nights on the sofa, roast dinners with distant family.

Of course, it stung when it ended.

Still, this was a different pain to previous break-ups.

In the past, the pain stemmed from wondering if I'd ever meet a woman like her again. I felt resistance to being single; desperation for affection.

Now, I knew I was a catch. I had the skillset to meet new girls and I'd kept it sharp throughout my relationship.

Even though I hadn't acted upon it, I knew how to capture a woman's interest and attract her. Plus, I had the excitement of a greyhound released from the traps.

These are the only attributes you need to secure a one-night stand.

Excitement plus confidence.

In spite of my broken heart, I pulled a nurse home from the nightclub on the day of the split, and a gloriously skinny pole-dancer two nights later.

It took me a year to get laid after my previous break-up. This time I managed to get two new girls in three days. What was the difference? First off, I accepted it was over. Olivia had become a different person to the one I fell in love with. Plus, when one person breaks another's heart, the dynamic changes between them forever. Even if couples get back together, their opinions of each other can never truly be the same. It's like starting a new relationship from scratch.

Secondly, I wasn't desperate for someone to replace Olivia. I thought it might take a while to get laid while I was still feeling sad. It'd also probably take months, if not years, to find another woman who was 'girlfriend material'. I accepted that and promised myself to enjoy meeting new women, regardless of who they were and what they thought of me.

This attitude attracts hotties like a boyband attracts prepubescent girls.

Sure, I was thinking about Olivia moments after these one-night stands got dressed, but that's better than thinking about her after a night of scaring women away with your neediness.

I knew these sad feelings would eventually fade. Having a naked pole dancer spread-eagled certainly speeds up the process.

5 attitude shifts to help you get over heartbreak

It's OK to not be OK: It can be frustrating when we don't feel better straight away, especially in this social media era when everyone around us appears to always be feeling fantastic.

It's biological to be upset after a break-up. Accept it's OK not to be OK. Shed some tears. Smash some plates. Grieve. Getting that negative energy out of you is the first step to feeling better.

This too shall pass: All emotions eventually fade. Time really does heal all wounds. Remember the previous time you were heartbroken and notice how silly that sadness seems now.

What doesn't kill you makes you stronger: Bodybuilding is about putting your muscles through so much strain that they break down. As they regenerate, they grow back strong enough to handle the pain next time. The heart is a muscle too, and it does exactly the same.

To become strong enough for an unbreakable relationship, you need to have been through emotional trauma. Each time it happens, you have the opportunity to dust yourself down , learn where you went wrong and become a better man.

This process is essential to becoming the man who can withstand the stresses of raising a family. How else are you meant to be able to maintain a healthy marriage while up all hours changing nappies? How can you become the father that supports his spouse and children in sickness and health?

It ain't over till the fat lady sings: All the best adventures have an unexpected plot twist before the good guy gets the girl. Those who take a break-up as an opportunity to become a better man tend to end up with an even better girlfriend.

All good things come to an end: Even the most eye-catching flowers eventually wilt and die, but that doesn't make them any less beautiful in the time they were alive. Sadly, most relationships end on a sour note too, but again this doesn't make the happy times any less special.

Every Oscar-winning film has an ending. So does every Shakespeare play, 80s power ballad and best-selling book. Celebrate what you created, then accept that it came to an end. Now, you can look forward to the next chapter of your romance tale.

10. WHY WOULD ANYONE PUT THEMSELVES THROUGH THIS?

At times, this process of 'teaching yourself sexy' will be the most uncomfortable thing you'll ever do.

If you follow the steps properly, you'll feel silly, scared and small. Your ego will be battered to the ground and shit on by tons of beautiful women.

Is that a price worth paying just to get more pussy? Absolutely, some would say! There's nothing unnatural about a young man wanting a ridiculous amount of sex.

Even if you're not so sure, the rewards of following this process extend way beyond an excessive sex life.

The thrill of the chase

The adrenaline before you approach a beautiful stranger. The challenge of overcoming her shit tests. The social freedom you feel when you reach 'flow state'. The epic adventures of getting a new woman from the bar to the bedroom. These are addictive experiences.

It may not be a better sensation than sex, nor more satisfying than that beautiful sticky gooey feeling of being in love, but these moments make you feel alive nonetheless.

Personal growth

Growing the balls to speak to a gorgeous woman. Being told to go fuck yourself. Finding a woman that likes you only to fuck it up. Dealing with cockblocks. Awkward first dates. Flakes.

On one hand, that all sounds really uncomfortable. Why not just wait for that woman at work who sort of likes you? On the other, it's these uncomfortable moments which make you a stronger man. It's here you develop that magnetic personality that everyone wants to be around.

This shit got me the best house I'd ever lived in. It's led me to some of my best friends. It helped me get the most fantastic girlfriend I'd ever had.

The alternative

The romantic path that most 'normal' people end up on is terrifying.

I see so many 'normal' men and women settle for partners they can't stand. They argue, they belittle each other, they boss each other around, yet still stay together. I swear it's because they're scared of being single. Sure, they might hate their spouse, but at least they're not lonely.

These couples stop trying to impress each other, safe in the knowledge that their other half can't do any better. Many end up having children. This sounds horrific as it is - the sleepless nights, tantrums, changing nappies, constant attention. The never-ending worrying whether it's OK, while it screams, shits itself and breaks your favourite possessions. Imagine doing it with some woman who annoys you, and maybe isn't even that hot anymore. No wonder the divorce rate is sky-high...

Of course, divorcing her will cost half your net worth, and maybe a huge battle to see these kids. Fancy jumping out of the melting pot into the fire?

I do want to start a family. I think all decent humans should. It's biological, although I see many logical reasons not to. It's therefore going to have to be with a human that's so awesome I'm willing to ignore all the flaws of monogamy. She'll have to be so perfect for me, that I'll believe we can beat the odds and have a happy family.

What are the chances of finding the perfect partner from a pool of Tinder matches and friends-of-friends? It's possible, but the odds are against you. The more women you can make yourself meet and the better you get at making incredible first impressions, the more likely you'll be to meet that perfect partner.

Typically, aiming for this higher tier of women will inspire you to dress better, get fitter, eat healthier and make more money. Most of the wingmen I've met eventually transform into well-dressed, fit, fashionable, entrepreneurial dudes. It's funny how that works. Jim Rohn says you become the average of the five people you surround yourself with. I reckon it's more to do with the type of guys you're competing with in the club...By following the steps in this book, you can outcompete the guy with good looks, status and money, but that's not to say having these things aren't awesome.

If every man learned to love the thrill of the chase, I reckon the marriage rate would drop. More men would be happier playing the field (or would at least wait longer to settle down). The divorce rate would probably plummet too, as men would be able to step up and make better romantic choices. More happy endings all round.

I'm a creep

I admit it. There's a lot of creepy shit in this story. Meeting strange introverts from the internet. Getting to the club at 21.00 to 'practice' hitting on women. Struggling through entire nights with no-one wanting to speak to me.

Still, the only thing creepier than learning how to pick up women is NOT learning how to pick up women. Dudes approaching chicks with no social acuity, from a place of scarcity and self-hate (assuming they were brave enough to approach at all), failing and heading home to scroll through porn and Plenty of Fish.

That's the path I was on. At best, I would have fallen into a co-dependent relationship with some woman. Any woman willing to put up with this pathetic behaviour. What path are you on?

Sure, the short-term awkwardness of being rejected or ignored feels creepy. It's nowhere near as creepy as the long-term problem of being stuck in your 40s, 50s or 60s, still unable to meet a good woman.

Thank goodness I stumbled across this 'strange' subculture. I've dated and slept with women I couldn't even imagine giving me the time of day. I'm well on my way to meeting that perfect partner. Plus, I've gained the social skills that helped gain me all sorts of other opportunities. The same can happen for you.

The final chapter includes some of the crazy sex experiences I've enjoyed since learning these skills. It highlights how much fun you can have while learning seduction.

However, it should be seen as more than a hobby. Mastering these skills will make you more fulfilled than anything else you'll ever learn. The alternative is you meet, marry and start a family with a mediocre woman (who, statistically, you'll end up divorcing).

Once you see this skill exists, there's no going back. You have two options.

- Tell yourself this book is bullshit and ignore all of its advice.
- Start improving yourself today and look forward to enjoying the fruits of your hard work.

Either way, I hope you enjoy the journey.

11. CRAZY SEX STORIES

Hands up if you've skipped straight to this chapter...

It's funny how blokes always want to skip straight ahead to the sex scenes, whereas women understand the build-up is just as important.

What follows are examples of the type of adventures that the skills in this book can allow you to have.

This sort of thing doesn't happen to me every night, but the better you get at meeting women, the more these crazy stories tend to manifest...

Reality TV Romance
My appearance on the Channel 4 show 'First Dates'.

So, what really happens on First Dates?

First off, there was no Fred Sireix. This was Season 2, before he was introduced.

I filled out the online application shortly after watching the first ever episode, making sure to mention I'd been dumped on Christmas Day.

The interview process started with a researcher calling and grilling me about my love life. This took over an hour. Then, I travelled to London for a lengthy on-camera interview that would be used on the show if I was chosen.

Finally, another researcher phoned to tell me they'd found the perfect match. They'd found Hannah.

The build-up

An email explained what would happen on the day:

- We'd get £50 towards the cost of the meal.

- 'Featured daters' should find the producers straight after dinner for their post-date interview.

- We'd all get a free cab ride to any London destination, but participants MUST NOT GET IN A TAXI TOGETHER (this was actually written in capitals).

Filming took place during my first weekend living in London. I was worried about being humiliated on national TV. One clever comment about me being bald, short or arrogant and the lads would never let me live it down.

These nerves died once I discovered we'd only be 'background daters'. Essentially, we'd be sat in the corner without a mic. My 15 minutes of fame torn away.

I still had to wait outside the restaurant in the rain for two hours before eating. Each dater was called one by one so they could film the walk to the front door. I was the last bloke to enter the restaurant. I asked the runner for her phone number while I was waiting.

"Concentrate on charming your date," she said.

The date

As previously mentioned, the researchers played down how beautiful Hannah was.

For research purposes, I stalked her on social media recently. She's married now. She proposed to him.

I was shown to the table where she was already sat. The chat flowed smoothly straight away.

I remember not understanding anything on the menu. We both ordered some weird, but delicious pork dish.

Hannah would laugh really loudly at my jokes. Other couples turned around a few times. Perhaps the producers would pick up on how funny I was and ask me back for a future episode...

Before pudding, I read her palm. I taught myself this skill hours earlier, so I'd have something interesting to do on TV. The 'love line' on her left hand began at her middle finger, which means she falls in love easily.

I sat next to her after the meal was done and whispered how we were a hotter couple than any of the fancy 'featured daters'. We went halves on the £150+ bill (That's starters, mains and drinks. Avoid Paternoster Chop House unless Channel 4 is supplementing your meal.)

The afterparty

The date went well, but how was I meant to take things further? This girl lived in Guildford, so there was a good chance I'd never see her again. That email didn't explain what background daters should do after dinner, so it was time to be daring. I grabbed Hannah's hand, pulled her past the producers and out the front doors. The taxi drivers waiting to offer our free ride shouted something, but we strode past them. Our hearts were racing.

We polished off a few beers at a nearby bar. We boasted about being the best-looking couple on the show. We cussed at the producers for not picking us. From there, it all gets a bit blurry. Before I knew it, we were on the train to party at The Clapham Grand.

Guys, a gazelle doesn't take his date to meet a pack of lions. DON'T EVER TAKE YOUR DATE TO A CLUB. There were dozens of creepy dudes there trying to touch her. Luckily, she turned down every dance.

As midnight approached, she mentioned her last train home left in ten minutes. I told her she was free to get it, but was also good to stay at mine. She didn't need inviting twice.

Within half an hour, we were back at the house. She said my bedroom looked like a crack den, but couldn't even finish the insult before we were ripping each other's clothes off.

I threw her on the bed and we got straight down to it. Foreplay was off the menu. That's what happens when you spend two hours waiting in the rain and eight hours on the date.

We exchanged numbers the next day and texted for ages, but never got round to meeting again. She lived a fair distance away. That was always going to make dating difficult.

Still, we'll always have that three-second cutaway of Series 2 Episode 5 to look back on.

Lessons learned:

- Don't be afraid to break the rules. None of this would have happened if we'd waited to see what the producers wanted.

- It's in capitals above. DON'T EVER TAKE YOUR DATE TO A CLUB.

- First Dates has the most wonderful staff, who are genuinely thrilled to help people find true love.

Bon Voyage, Shoreditch

My crazy one-night stand with a hipster, hours before she left the country.

My first ever night out in Shoreditch.

A Friday night out with Chris, a 40-something accountant who I met at my first-ever Saturday Sarge. He had mastered the skill of speaking endlessly, even if I struggled to understand his deep Glaswegian accent.

He was giving me the grand tour of this trendy East London town. We finished up at Zigfrid Von Udderbelly - a small tiki bar that plays house music in Hoxton Square.

As soon as I set foot inside, I saw her. Tall, skinny, absolutely stunning.

She was queueing at the bar with no-one standing within ten feet of her. I stood beside her, but couldn't bring myself to open my mouth.

Sixty seconds passed. This girl looked so bored. She was alone. There was literally no excuse not to say hello.

My mind had gone blank. When you're really nervous and your heart rate escalates, blood flows out of your brain into other muscles, so it's tougher to think, not that this is a suitable excuse to stand there like an idiot.

Suddenly, Chris swooped in from the side. He introduced himself. The girl was instantly hooked. They grabbed cocktails and nestled into the corner of the bar. They'd stay there for the next hour or so.

The fact he snatched her so effortlessly made this a lesson that didn't need teaching twice. JUST. SAY. SOMETHING.

Getting shot down by a beautiful girl feels nowhere near as soul-destroying as staying silent and watching someone else get her. I still remember the cheeky smirk on Chris' stupid face as he led her to the front doors and back to his flat.

The hipster girls

Alone in the bar feeling somewhat sorry for myself, I spotted two trendy women sipping mojitos.

The brunette wore a trilby and a black-patterned playsuit. The huge flowered tattoo on her back might as well have been a bouquet. Her mascara was running as if she'd been crying. The blonde was dressed equally quirkily.

They were in pretty intense conversation. Some serious drama must have went down, but I wasn't going to hesitate again.

"You guys definitely look like you're from Shoreditch."

They looked confused and slightly pissed off to be interrupted.

"I think it's the trilby; it looks really edgy and alternative."

I told them some fake story about being refused entry for being too mainstream and how the bouncers were more interested in scanning my iTunes than my ID.

The brunette was surprisingly receptive to my bullshit. My enthusiasm for Shoreditch must have been infectious. She explained how she was leaving her dull-sounding office job for some six-month charity project in Africa. Something about building a school for starving children.

This was her leaving party. There were dozens of workmates with her at the bar, but only the blonde remained. She'd gone to the bar to grab drinks. As we took a seat, I asked whether she'd been crying. Apparently, her manager, who she'd previously been shagging, was caught snogging some other whore she worked with.

The blonde (her best mate) saw it, started shouting and screaming, and that's supposedly why loads of people left early. (Unsurprising. The blonde looked like the confrontational type. She didn't even giggle at my iTunes gag).

Brunette started to open up about how she was 'done with all fake bitches who live in London'. I cheered her up with stories about all the 'genuine bitches' I knew.

"You're an idiot, but you have really nice eyes," she said.

We kissed soon after. It was clear this girl was up for some sort of angry revenge sex.

Half an hour later, the blonde staggered over, looking worse for wear. Some dude had been plying her with too many free drinks. We went to grab food, but the blonde took ten minutes to complete the 200-metre journey to the burger joint. I've seen women on crutches walk faster...Brunette planned to grab a taxi to Surrey Quays but wanted to make sure her mate got on the bus to Liverpool Street safely.

Bus stop drama

We made it to the bus stop after batting away dozens of creepy drunk dudes catcalling the girls.

Brunette kept complaining about the cold. Blonde had been distracted by some sketchy drug-dealer. My heart sank as the bus left without her.

Twelve minutes until the next one. Brunette wouldn't shut up about the weather. Blonde started shouting how I looked like her dad. I was beginning to hate both of them.

The next bus turned up, but the blonde was now busy being hit on by some other hipsters. Once again, it drove off without her.

I'd had enough of this. When the next bus came, I fireman-carried her towards it. She couldn't find her Oyster card, so I swiped mine. She took a seat once the brunette told her she was fine being left with me.

From there, it was straightforward. I kept chatting about African schoolchildren and how she better remember to build the cafeteria. I assumed she'd let me stay over. We thumbed down a cab to Surrey Quays and I jumped in.

She led me into a bare-looking bedroom surrounded by open suitcases. The sex was terrible. Super non-romantic and rushed. To be fair, it was past 4.30am by the time we got down to it.

We were woken up really early by the brunette's mobile phone. She'd received a fair few missed calls from the hussy who'd snogged her boss. (I'd had a couple of gloating texts from Chris, cheeky git).

Brunette kicked me out of bed because she had a goodbye breakfast booked with her mum.

I enquired whether the blonde had got in touch.

"Don't worry, she wasn't too drunk to get on that bus. She just really hated you."

Funny that, as the bus I put her on didn't even go to Liverpool Street! I told her London would miss her and set off on an early-morning mission home.

Lessons learned:

- JUST SAY SOMETHING to a woman you fancy. Nothing hurts worse than not talking to her and watching your mate take her home instead.

- Before you head home alone, try chatting up one more woman. You never know what might happen

- Try and win over a woman's friends if you can. It makes taking her home around twenty times easier.

The American Virgin

Taking a pure and innocent tourist on a tour of the capital

When I arrived in London, I assumed every nightclub would be busy every night. After all, this is our capital city and the most popular tourist destination on Earth.

Not so. You have to be clued up to know what clubs are good on weekdays. Even then, the clientele is mostly students and tourists.

My wingmen and I joke that we should get a cap every time we turn up to Zoo Bar on a school night, because we're the only people representing England.

This might have actually been the case on a Wednesday evening back in July 2014.

The dance floor was dead. We were amusing this huge group of American teenagers in the smoking area. Mostly jokes about Justin Bieber and how Jägerbomb is the national beverage of Britain.

They thought we were idiots, but we were cracking ourselves up and there was no-one better to talk to. I spotted this tiny shy blonde whose bright blue eyes would light up whenever I'd crack a stupid comment.

"How come you're so quiet?" I asked obnoxiously.

We started chatting separately. Her group was on a college trip. They were only in the country for another seven days. I recommended some cool stuff going on in the capital that week.

All of her mates decided to head home, but she stayed in the smoking area with me. It was only then that I clocked she might be into me (shy girls can't flirt for shit). Unfortunately, there was this equally short, equally shy, emo-looking guy who wouldn't leave her side.

With every flirty statement she laughed at, I could see his inner torment. I imagine he's written a love poem to her in knife on his arm.

I walked them to the bus stop. Her eyes were lit up like Bambi's, but things would go no further while this emo was in orbit. She couldn't remember her English phone number, so I had to settle for her surname and attempt to find her on Facebook.

I shot her a short message saying I'd be at Zoo Bar again on Monday but didn't hold much hope of hearing back.

The tour of London

I'd forgotten about her by the time Monday arrived. Once again, I was chatting shit to some tourist in the smoking area when I felt a tap on my shoulder.

This tiny teenage tourist ditched all of her friends in a foreign country to find me (she'd sent a message beforehand, but I didn't read it).

I'd give her a tour of London she'd never forget.

She says she's never eaten fish and chips, so we buy some and eat them in Trafalgar Square. I teach her about grime. Wiley blasts through my iPhone 4 speakers. She says she prefers country music.

I make some excuse about an afterparty at my house. This was back before I knew the quickest route home, so we took TWO nightbuses.

I may have exaggerated the time it takes to get to Tooting. On the second bus, she starts to look a bit concerned. She shows me her favourite country songs on Spotify and we sing along. I teach her a bit more about UK rap music. Anything to take her mind off the length of this trip.

Of course, everyone is asleep once we get home. I blame the bus driver for going so slowly. We head upstairs and share our first kiss. I try to take things further, but she's visibly uncomfortable. To my shock, she explains she's a VIRGIN and isn't ready for this sort of thing.

Awkward silence. Already drained from entertaining her on two nightbuses, I don't even try to change her mind.

You should lose your V-plates to someone who loves you, not some idiot who tries to teach you N-Dubz lyrics on the nightbus. So I walk her back to the bus stop and wait for the N155 to arrive.

I feel guilty. This poor girl won't be home until past 5.00am. That's if she finds her way back at all. I think about retiring the afterparty line. But just before I get to bed, she sends the most adorable Facebook message.

Hey, I just wanted to thank you for a really fun night and apologize for leading you on I suppose. Were I not still a virgin I would have happily stayed the night. Honestly sometimes I wish I could just get it out of the way so I wasn't such a buzz kill in situations like that. Anyway, thanks again - you're the best 😊

Lessons learned:

- Tourists love being taken on adventures, even if they only involve chips and a nightbus.

- When a shy woman eventually opens up, it's the most wonderful experience. A bit like watching a boring caterpillar turn into a beautiful butterfly.

- Don't use the 'afterparty' excuse to pull virgins. They might think that's actually why you're heading home together.

Russians In A Strip Club

This story is too sexy to stay in Vegas.

I travelled to Las Vegas to volunteer at a week-long Real Social Dynamics dating and self-development seminar.

All attendees had access to this nightclub promoter who'd text us a list of clubs we could enter for free. We were also invited to a daily afterparty at Sapphire, which is the world's largest strip club.

On the third night, I went to a medium-sized club called The Bank with a couple of dudes I'd met at the seminar. I'd struck it lucky in the casinos, but not with the women. The previous night I'd mistakenly gone home with a hooker, so was keen to make amends.

Towards the end of the evening, I spotted these two women looking bored at the bar. One was old and brunette. The other was skinny and blonde.

They were Russian. The only Russian word I knew was 'da' (yes). I'd soon learn 'nyet' (no).

A third friend staggered over. She was super-glamorous, but definitely super-drunk. She'd fall over her feet and keep calling me Johnny.

The lights came on. I felt like they didn't know me well enough to head back to Excalibur (my hotel). In fact, the skinny blonde had barely said a word.

So instead, I explained about the awesome afterparty and how the promoter would send a limousine to take us there. I failed to mention it was at a strip club...

I spoke with the skinny blonde while waiting for the limo to arrive. On the ride to Sapphire, we took selfies and she showed off photos of the bodybuilding competitions she used to compete in. She was the one I wanted.

The afterparty was three times busier than the club, but it was just strippers and dudes. The women were visibly intimidated. Skinny blonde was back in her shell. Super-drunk ranted about how none of the strippers were even hot. We left after one champagne.

This trio was as noisy as ever in the cab home. They saw Sapphire as a funny story, rather than a night-ruiner. Super-drunk almost fell out the door at her stop.

"Lovely to meet you, Johnny!" she shrieked.

I told the other two I'd teach them to play roulette. My plan was to play until old brunette goes to bed, then work some magic with skinny blonde. Just keep spinning that wheel and praying I don't bankrupt myself.

The plan backfired before it even began. Turns out these Russians were sharing a room. What's more, while old brunette was bang up for roulette, skinny blonde wanted to go to bed.

A million options flicked through my mind. Could I convince the brunette to go to the casino alone? Should I try for a threesome? Neither seemed like a simple option, especially as skinny blonde was almost asleep. For a former body-builder, she didn't have much stamina.

I ended up taking old brunette to the roulette tables. We won twenty bucks by betting on black, but this was now looking like a third night without any pink.

She walked me to the main exit. I pointed out Excalibur.

"You'd love it there," I said.

"Why?"

"Because there's a big bottle of Smirnoff in my room."

She was up for it. Not until now had I thought about banging old brunette. At 04.30 on a Wednesday morning, it would be funnier than not doing it.

After the short stroll to my hotel room, we downed a shot of Smirnoff and things escalated from there.

Honestly, it was awkward at best. Her body was below par even for a thirty-something. She insisted we kept the lights off and kept giggling nervously like a girl half her age. We stopped twice so she could swig another vodka shot. I was thinking about the Sapphire strippers through most of it. Even so, this was the best game of Russian Roulette I'd ever played.

Lessons learned:

- Even the quietest club nights can spark the wildest adventures

- Always ask a girl where and with whom she is staying

- Russians will follow you anywhere if there's vodka

My Date Got Hit By A Bus
She turned up in Tooting straight from the hospital

Daygame is a beautiful thing when done properly. At this point, it was still an art I'd rarely been brave enough to engage in.

When I spotted this tall blonde waiting for a bus, it seemed like the perfect opportunity to try.

Her legs were so skinny. Her hair so straight, long and shiny. Her skin was so fair. It was as if God created a Barbie doll and sent her to wait for the 8 towards Bow Church. There was not a soul stood within ten feet of her.

I strolled over and told her she looked really nice (just like Jake had taught me some time ago). She thanked me in this deep Scandinavian accent, which I correctly guessed was from Sweden.

I teased how she looked like a cliché Swede (hot and blonde). I told her the only Swedish I knew was 'Elskling' (darling) and 'Julmust' (some festive beverage). We exchanged numbers and she agreed to come to Tooting the next day.

The accident

That morning, she texted to say she'd been knocked off her motorbike by a bus.

Was this the world's most dramatic excuse to flake on a date? I asked if she was OK. A couple of hours later, she replied claiming the doctor had checked her out and she was cool to come on the date after all.

There's no way that was true? Surely, she must have gotten cold feet, then had a change of heart?

My shortest ever date

I met her at Tooting Broadway and tried to hug her. She cringed, as if my hands were a cold shower. She was still a little fragile from the bus accident...

It was true!? She told me what happened and how the doctor insisted there was no long-term damage.

We sat in the beer garden closest to the tube because walking was still a bit painful for her.

I was my usual funny self, but she was wincing in pain with every punchline.

She asked me to make fewer jokes because laughing really hurts her ribs.

At this point, I couldn't imagine she'd be that adventurous in bed. (This thought actually went through my head. I'm going to hell).

Most of the conversation was steered around her motorbike and the bus colliding into her. (No risk of her finding that funny.)

About 20 minutes into the date, she told me her painkillers were wearing off. The agony and sorrow in her eyes made it clear she needed to leave.

We walked 200 metres to the tube station, did an awkward half-hug that still sort of hurt her, and away she hobbled.

The worst date ever. We never saw each other again. She didn't even reply my texts. Maybe she died?

Lessons learned:

- Hitting on girls in the street is awesome

- Sometimes girls have a genuinely good reason to cancel a date

- She's definitely not dead. I recently checked her WhatsApp and she's changed her profile picture since we met. Maybe I should text her?

For more stories like this, subscribe to Joe's email newsletter at www.thelondondater.co.uk/dates

Made in the USA
Columbia, SC
06 March 2019